MW01196204

This journal belongs to:

Made in the USA
Las Vegas, NV
09 February 2022

43516058R00085